JAH TUFF'S

Worldwide

Reggae Festival

Guide

Ras Rolo

Copyright © 2014 (Revised & Edited for 2017) by Jah Tuff and RMCBooks. All rights reserved. Printed in the United States. The book author retains sole copyright to his contributions of this book. No part of this publication may be reproduced or distributed in any form or by any means without prior written consent from the author.

Editor: Ginny Greene
Cover Design: Ras Rolo

Contact info:
twitter: @JahTuff
email: mixtaloopz@gmail.com

ISBN-13: 978-0-9840186-9-7
ISBN-10: 0984018697

The purpose of this guide is to honor and promote reggae and dancehall music and to highlight all of the incredible music festivals around the world, and is not associated with any specific festival, concert or event. Reggae music is the healing of the nation, and togetherness is righteousness. So unite as one people, spread positive vibes and enjoy the numerous reggae music festivals held each year while supporting your favorite reggae and dancehall artists who create the music that we love.

~ Give thanks & praises to the most high, Jah Rastafari, Haile Selassie I ~

~ Table of Contents ~

1. January Music Festivals 4-5
2. February Music Festivals 5-7
3. March Music Festivals 7
4. April Music Festivals 8
5. May Music Festivals 9-11
6. June Music Festivals 11-16
7. July Music Festivals 16-23
8. August Music Festivals 23-29
9. September Music Festivals 29-30
10. October Music Festivals 30
11. November Music Festivals 31
12. December Music Festivals 31-32
13. Reggae Festivals Chart 33-42
14. Origins of Reggae Music 43-45

Charitable Reggae Organizations 46
Protecting Africa's Elephants 47
Irie Reggae Resources 48
Listing of Reggae Artists 49-58

JANUARY

Shaggy & Friends – 1st weekend January (Kingston, Jamaica) ~ This annual charity concert raises money for the Bustamante Children's Hospital in Jamaica. The *Shaggy Make a Difference Foundation* has raised & donated over $90 million dollars in proceeds to the hospital which buys much needed medical equipment and is helping to establish the cardiac wing of the hospital through its partnership with *Chain of Hope Jamaica*. This event draws award-winning reggae & dancehall artists to support the cause. https://www.facebook.com/shaggyandfriends

Rebel Salute – 3rd weekend January (St. Ann Parish, Jamaica) ~ One of Jamaica's largest reggae festivals, Rebel Salute is a '*must see*' on the live music events calendar and is a staple of Jamaican culture. It provides delicious vegetarian-only food options, is an alcohol-free, drug-free, violence-free event, and features the best reggae & dancehall performers in Jamaica both upcoming and veteran. This conscious roots music festival is held every year around promoter Tony Rebel's earthstrong (birthday) January 15th, and embodies the warm tropical weather and hospitality of Jamaica. https://www.facebook.com/rebelsalutejamaica

Jamaican Jazz & Blues Festival – 4th weekend January (Kingston, Montego Bay & Trelawny, Jamaica) ~ The top entertainers from around the world gather for this premiere annual event spread out among three various locations on the beautiful island of Jamaica. It encompasses a variety of music genres including jazz, blues, reggae, R&B, soca, Latin and fusion and attracts more than 30,000 people every year. https://www.facebook.com/jamaicajazzandblues

Panama Reggae Jam Music Festival – 4th weekend January (Panama City, Panama) ~ Dubz Reggae Production brings a new venue on the reggae circuit which is sure to grow in size and popularity. Located at Latitude 47 in Panama City, this festival hosts local and international reggae and dub artists as well as world-class DJ's. http://allevents.in/panama%20city/panama-reggae-jam-music-festival-2015-sab-31-de-enero-latitude-47-calle-uruguay/718522664930332#

FEBRUARY

Bob Marley Birthday Bash – 1st weekend February (Negril, JA) ~ This annual reggae event is held in the 'Capital of Casual' Negril Jamaica, and celebrates the King of Reggae Bob Marley. BMBB attracts the best international reggae, dancehall and world music artists, includes the finest authentic selection of Jamaican & Caribbean foods, arts & crafts vendors, and offers a variety of festival and cultural activities such as drumming & Jankunoo dancers. https://www.facebook.com/BobMarleyBirthdayBash

Dub Champions Festival – 1st weekend February (Amsterdam & Vienna) ~ Founded by Subatomic Sound, *Dub Champions* is an incredible show featuring 20+ legendary dub music artists and the hottest sounds systems in the world. This music genre combines reggae roots dub with futuristic bass sounds that create this unique niche in the reggae music industry. It is a three-day event held in two different locations in Europe, offers Caribbean & international cuisine, t-shirt vendors, and is growing in popularity every year. http://www.dubchampions.com/

One Love Festival – 1st weekend February (Tauranga, New Zealand) ~ Produced by PATO Entertainment Camp, One Love Festival hosts the best roots reggae, urban, soul and world music performers. Located on the picturesque Bay of Plenty in New Zealand, this two-day event is a co-celebration of Waitangi Day and Bob Marley's birthday and offers a variety of regional and international cuisines, festival activities, camping & vending. http://onelovefestival.co.nz/

9 Mile Music Festival – 2nd weekend February (Miami, FL) ~ This reggae festival was pioneered by Bob Marley's mother, Cedella Marley Booker, and started as a labor of love. Its mission is to give back to the community, and is committed to doing good deeds and spreading love. Along with admission, four canned goods are required for entry and are distributed to shelters in Miami & Jamaica. http://ninemileent.com/

Tribute to the Reggae Legends – Presidents Day, February (San Diego, CA) ~ Formerly known as *Bob Marley Day*, this music festival is spearheaded by WorldBeat Productions and is one of Southern California's largest Reggae events. The festival hosts an incredible lineup of new and veteran reggae & dancehall artists, and was founded by Makeda Dread – a personal friend of Bob Marley. After he passed in 1981, she decided to create a tribute to Bob Marley Festival which is now 33 years strong. https://www.facebook.com/tributetothereggaelegends

Blue Mountain Music Festival – 3rd weekend February (Holywell, Jamaica) ~ Set atop the rolling hills of Holywell, Jamaica, The Blue Mountain Music Festival is where reggae music, art, culture & nature come together. This two-day event features a variety of musical performances as well as camping, hiking, outdoor adventures and other cultural activities. https://www.facebook.com/bluemountainmusicfestival

Oneness Reggae Fest – 3rd weekend February (Rio Nuevo Village, St. Mary, Jamaica) ~ This irie reggae festival promotes 'Peace, Love & Unity through positive & spiritual vibrations'. With it's slogan "Out of Many One Music". It showcases various reggae & dancehall artists, Caribbean food vendors, and emphasizes the positive roots & culture that represent the island of Jamaica. http://onenessreggaefest.com/

Ragga Muffins Festival – 3rd & 4th weekend February (Long Beach, CA & Bay Area, CA) ~ Ragga Muffin Productions & Moss Jacobs host this annual two-day reggae concert in SoCal & the Bay Area featuring the best in reggae and dancehall music. Also formerly part of the *Bob Marley Day* festival tour, this event celebrates Bob Marley, reggae culture & Jamaican cuisine. http://www.raggamuffinsfestival.com/

MARCH

MoonSplash – 2nd weekend March (Dune Preserve, Anguilla) ~ The Eastern Caribbean's pioneer of reggae music, Bankie Banx hosts the Moonsplash Music Festival each year on the island of Anguilla. Located on Rendezvous Bay, Bankie runs a restaurant, night club and beach bar called The Dune Preserve and provides an intimate stage for reggae veterans as well as up & coming singers. http://olaidebanks.wix.com/moonsplash

APRIL

Austin Reggae Festival – 3rd weekend April (Austin, TX) ~ Deep in the heart of Texas, this annual outdoor event celebrates the coming of spring and the unity of all people through conscious music. Hosting the best reggae & world music artists, ARF donates proceeds to the Capital Area Food Bank which helps alleviate hunger in Austin and surrounding communities. It is located downtown in Butler Park, easily accessible on foot, bicycle, or the Capital MetroRail. http://austinreggaefest.com/

Easter Reggae Showcase – 3rd weekend April (Brixton, London) ~ Held in jolly ole London England, this concert features an incredible line up of reggae artists that represent the Studio One & Treasure Isle Label. Each performer offers insight into their musical careers, live performances, and hits they have recorded. http://www.o2academybrixton.co.uk/event/63641/the-easter-reggae-showcase-2014-tickets

Barbados Reggae Festival – 4th week April (various locations, Barbados) ~ Produced by Digicel, this reggae festival showcases local, regional and world-class reggae & dancehall artists. Barbados Reggae Festival is a week-long event that provides Caribbean & international cuisine, various market vendors, cultural activities and attracts visitors from around the world. www.thebarbadosreggaefestival.com

Dis Poem Word Festival – 4th weekend April (Portland, Jamaica) ~ This day-long event encompasses dub poetry, agricultural awareness & spoken word entertainment. The proceeds go to the RAS Takura Scholarship fund which supports students at the College of Agriculture, Science and Education in Portland. https://www.facebook.com/dispoemwordznagrofestival

MAY

Freedom Sounds Ska & Reggae Festival – 1st weekend May (Cologne, Germany) ~ *Reggae Steady Ska* presents this irie two-day festival that features the best of both ska & reggae music. It also includes a short-film festival shown at a local cinema in Cologne highlighting the most influential Ska & Reggae films.
http://www.freedomsoundsfestival.de/

Reggae on the Bay – 1st weekend May (Chaguaramas, Trinidad) ~ Hennessey Artistry hosts one of the Caribbean's premiere reggae festivals, showcasing world-class reggae artists on the island of Trinidad from the amphitheater in beautiful O2 Park. This incredible open-air event offers Caribbean & international cuisine, arts & crafts vendors and various festival activities.
http://triniscene.com/tsv7/home/

SoCal World Music Festival – 2nd weekend May (San Diego, CA) ~ This event offers three days of irie roots reggae music, Jamaican cuisine, vendors and easy-access camping. They also have reggae/dancehall DJ's spinning tunes until 2am, prize giveaways and various activities for the entire family.
https://www.facebook.com/SoCalWorldMusicFestival

Gambia International Roots Festival – 2nd – 3rd weekends May (Gambia, Africa) ~ This international roots festival was created to encourage people of African descent to 'further discover, re-affirm and re-embrace' their ancestral identity. In addition to hosting top African & reggae artists, this cultural festival includes traditional music & dance, African cuisine, a carnival procession featuring masquerades of different ethnic groups, historical narratives and meetings with village elders & chiefs.
http://rootsgambia.gm/

Buckroe Beach Reggae Festival – 3rd weekend May (Hampton, VA) ~ BBRC was started in 2010 funded by grass roots efforts, and is now one of the premiere reggae festivals on the East Coast. This celebration of unity & culture is located on the shores of Chesapeake Bay, and attracts an array of local, regional & international reggae artists. http://www.bbreggaefest.com/

Best of the Best International Music Festival – 4th weekend May (Miami, FL) ~ One of the premiere music festivals in North America, Best of the Best features the top reggae, hip hop, R&B, soca music artists today. Producers Rockers Island & Massive B celebrate seven years of success with this annual event, which is set in beautiful downtown Miami Bayfront Park overlooking the waters of Biscayne Bay. http://bestofthebestconcert.com/

California Roots Festival – 4th weekend May (Monterey, CA) ~ The Monterey County Fair & Event Center host this annual festival that features legendary reggae & world music artists and promotes the importance of environmental awareness. It includes a festival vendor area, various international cuisines, live painters, yoga, meditation, and other cultural activities. http://californiarootsfestival.com/

Camp Reggae – 4th weekend May (Turtle Town, TN) ~ This annual three-day camp hosts local, regional and international reggae artists high in the scenic Smoky Mountains of Tennessee. It offers Jamaican, international and regional food options, drum circles, yoga, soccer and various camp activities. http://www.campreggae.org/

Four Roses Kentucky Reggae Festival – 4ᵗʰ weekend May (Louisville, KY) ~ Louisville's hottest Memorial Day Weekend event showcasing the best local & regional reggae bands. Located at the Louisville Water tower, this riverfront venue offers Jamaican & Caribbean cuisine, arts & crafts vendors and cultural activities, and dedicated to promoting peace & unity among all people. http://www.kentuckyreggaefestival.com/

UCLA Jazz Reggae Festival – 4ᵗʰ weekend May (Los Angeles, CA) ~ Held on the Intramural Field at UCLA, this two-day outdoor venue is a celebration of music, art, food & culture, and features the hottest reggae, dancehall, jazz, R&B and soca artists today. Founded and produced by students of UCLA, this event promotes peace & unity among all cultures and environmental awareness. http://www.jazzreggaefest.com/#welcome

JUNE

City of Trees Reggae Music Festival – 1ˢᵗ weekend June (Sacramento, CA) ~ This irie festival is held in California's state capital Sacramento, and attracts the best reggae & dancehall artists from around the world. It supports local artists & businesses, provides international foods & vendors, and is a true 'for the people, by the people' grassroots experience. https://www.facebook.com/cityoftreesreggaemusicfestival

Jamming Festival – 1ˢᵗ weekend June (Bogota, Columbia) ~ Promoting 'Music, Culture & Peace', Bogota's Jamming Festival boasts some of the top reggae, ska and dancehall artists of today. This venue offers cultural, recreational and festival activities, a vendor marketplace as well as Caribbean, Latin American and International cuisine. http://www.jammingfestival.com.co/

Riddim Festival Aalborg – 1st weekend June (Aalborg, Denmark) ~ New on the concert circuit, *Riddim Festival* showcases an array of music genres including reggae, dancehall, hip-hop, jazz, funk, dubstep, drum & bass, Afrobeats, jungle etc. This event is dedicated to positive vibes and making the world a better place by combining music, art, language and culture. https://www.facebook.com/Riddimfestival

RUHR Reggae Summer Festival – 1st weekend June (Dortmund, Germany) ~ One of the biggest music festivals in Europe that features various genres of music including reggae, dancehall, dub, ska, hip-hop and more. Enjoy three days of peace, love & music including Caribbean, European & international cuisine, market vendors and various festival activities. http://www.ruhr-reggae-summer.de/

Reggae in the Desert – 2nd weekend June (Las Vegas, NV) ~ The largest reggae festival in Las Vegas that features legendary reggae performances and promotes the unifying power of reggae music & Caribbean lifestyle. Reggae in the Desert includes a vendor market area, arts & crafts, Jamaican & international foods and an indoor VIP section that provides complimentary snacks, drinks, wine, and air conditioning that provides relief from the heat. http://www.reggaeinthedesert.com/

Reggae in the Hills – 2nd weekend June (Angel's Camp, CA) ~ This three-day festival is located on 80 acres of open fairgrounds and features top local, regional and international reggae artists. It provides an incredible selection of Jamaican, international and local organic foods, a vendor market, camping, skate park, disc golf, live painting & other activities. http://reggaeinthehills.com/

Aarhus Reggae Festival – 3rd weekend June (Aarhus, Denmark) ~ A two-day musical celebration showcasing the diverse culture of Denmark, the Aarhus Reggae Festival hosts some of the top reggae and dancehall artists from around the world. This venue provides festival activities, arts & crafts, a vendor market area as well as Caribbean, European & international cuisine. http://www.aarhusreggaefest.com/

Central Florida International Reggae Festival – 3rd weekend June (Orlando, FL) ~ This world-class reggae festival is a tribute concert to the King of Reggae Bob Marley and his contributions to our lives. Located in beautiful Orlando Festival Park, *CFL Reggae Fest* combines the best reggae music, art and culture with the best Jamaican, Caribbean & international food vendors, and offers various festival activities and provides a fun-filled day for friends and family. https://www.facebook.com/CFLreggaefest

Conscious Culture Festival – 3rd weekend June (Tonasket, WA) ~ This irie festival combines music, art & environmental awareness, and showcases 4 stages, over 80 performers spanning a variety of music genres including reggae, rock, folk, blues, soul, hip-hop, dubstep, house and more. Dedicated to recycling, CCF offers tent camping, arts & crafts, a beer garden, live glass blowing, a kids area, and workshops including yoga, Tai Chi and African drumming. http://www.consciousculturefestival.com/

Omaha Solstice Reggae & World Music Festival – 3rd weekend June (Omaha, NE) ~ Promoting unity and music appreciation, this concert combines a variety of music genres including reggae, rock steady, ska & world music. It also offers numerous market vendors, Jamaican & international cuisine, massage therapy & various cultural activities for the kids. http://www.omahasolsticereggaefest.com/

Sierra Nevada World Music Festival (SNWMF) – 3rd weekend June (Mendocino, CA) ~ Epiphany Artists hosts this annual 'summer solstice & world peace' celebration, and showcases renowned reggae, dancehall & world music performers. It is located at the irie Mendocino County Fairgrounds in Anderson Valley, and provides a festival village with international cuisine, vendor market, arts & crafts, camping & RV's, children's activities and a late-night dancehall DJ tent. www.snwmf.com

Ziontific Summer Solstice Music Festival – 3rd weekend June (Stockbridge, VT) ~ This annual event features the best local and regional reggae artists, as well as offers a great selection of international and organic foods. *Ziontific* boasts an array of festival amenities such as tubing, swimming, fire shows, Tai Chi, yoga, massage, meditation, singing workshops, a wellness village and a 'KidZone'. http://www.ziontificproductions.com/

Couleur Café Festival – 4th weekend June (Brussels, Belgium) ~ One of the most anticipated shows in Europe, this three-day urban music festival features reggae, dub, electronic, Latin, hip-hop, funk & soul artists. It provides a relaxing campsite oasis, a large food court with over 50 world kitchens offering the finest Caribbean & international cuisine, and proceeds from this event support social & educational projects for Belgium & other countries abroad. http://www.couleurcafe.be/

Groovin' in the Park – 4th weekend June (Jamaica, Queens NY) ~ One of the best summer concerts in New York, *Groovin in the Park* is held at Roy Wilkins Recreational Park and features award-winning reggae and R&B performances. This cultural experience also includes Caribbean & international cuisine, a vendor market, and is a great experience for the entire family. www.groovininthepark.com

Reggae in the Trees – 4th weekend June (Selma, OR) ~ This all-ages, two-day festival is held in beautiful Southern Oregon that features some of the best local, regional and international reggae artists. It provides a vendor market area, arts & crafts, as well as a great selection of Jamaican, Caribbean & local organic foods. http://reggaeinthetrees.webs.com/

St. Kitts Music Festival – 4th week June (St. Kitts, WI) ~ The most diverse music festival in the Caribbean, this three-day event showcases legendary reggae artists from around the world and promotes local talent as well. Held on beautiful St. Kitts, it features a variety of music genres including dancehall, R&B, hip-hop, funk & world music as well as Caribbean & international cuisine, market vendors, cultural activities and arts & crafts. https://www.facebook.com/stkittsmusicfestival

Sumol Summer Fest – 4th weekend June (Ericeira, Portugal) ~ The largest reggae festival in Portugal, this beachside venue hosts the top reggae, dub & dancehall artists of today. This two-day irie event offers shuttles to the show, a skate park, market vendors & store, international foods, festival activities & projects, beach swimming and a welcome party the day before the show. http://www.sumolsummerfest.com/

Uplift Music & Arts Festival – 4th weekend June (Greenfield, NH) ~ Featuring the finest artists, musicians & international cuisine, this community-driven event is growing larger every year. Located just 1.5 hours north of Boston, *Uplift Music & Arts Festival* is family-friendly venue, and focuses on uplifting the community through a 'music & arts-based event'. http://www.upliftapparel.com

Woodbury Reggae Festival – 4th weekend June (Woodbury, CT) ~ This is one of the premiere roots rock reggae festivals on the East Coast which is now 42 years strong, and still features the best in reggae & world music. It is located in the majestic hills of Woodbury, CT and provides local & international cuisine, arts & crafts, market vendors, also activities including tubing, swimming, zip lining, hiking, picnicking and camping. http://www.woodburyskiarea.com/summer/concerts.html

JULY

Festival Musa Cascais – 1st weekend July (Cascais, Portugal) ~ This reggae music festival is one of the largest in Portugal, and features some of the best reggae and world music performers. It offers international foods & drink, market vendors and camping, and emphasizes unity, positive vibrations and environmental awareness. www.festivalmusa.org

Houston Caribbean Festival – 1st week July (Houston TX) ~ This annual event is a celebration of Caribbean & Latin culture featuring live reggae, soca & latin music. As the sounds of steel drums play in the background, enjoy arts & crafts, Caribbean & Latin cuisine, arts & craft vendors, various activities and a cultural costume parade. http://houstoncaribbeanfestival.com/

International Festival of Life – 1st week July (Chicago, IL) ~ Since 1993, the IFOL is dedicated to the unity of all people with its dual themes of "Living Together As One" & "Bringing Nations Together". This annual event showcases top reggae and world music performers, and includes vendors, arts & crafts, local & international foods, games and other cultural activities. http://martinsinterculture.com/ifol.html

International Reggae Day – 1st day July (Kingston, Jamaica) ~ IRD celebrates the best of Jamaican creativity, music & culture, and its positive influence on the world while showcasing legendary reggae artists. This event recognizes reggae music as the world's 'first true global beat' and Bob Marley as the world's first musical superstar. http://www.ireggaeday.com/

Lakesplash Festival – 1st weekend July (Bern, Switzerland) ~ Spreading positive vibes since 1998, this legendary open-air music event is one of the longest running shows in Europe. It is located in the village of Twann on beautiful Lake Biel in scenic Switzerland, offers numerous festival and local activities, and hosts some of the top reggae & world music artists today. http://www.lakesplash.ch/

Montenegro Sun Reggae Festival – 1st weekend July (Petrovac, Montenegro) ~ This summer music festival in Montenegro features top local, regional & international reggae artists including DJ's, local radio hosts and various sound systems. It includes Caribbean & international cuisine, vendor booths, arts & crafts, activities and an opening ceremony Zumba Party. www.facebook.com/MontenegroSunReggaeFestival?ref=stream

SummerJam Festival – 1st weekend July (Cologne, Germany) ~ One of the biggest annual festivals in Europe, SummerJam is a favorite venue for reggae & dancehall artists and attracts over 30,000 concert-goers from around the world. This three-day irie event promotes peace & unity with its "Share your Love" theme, and offers an incredible selection of Jamaican, Caribbean and regional foods, market vendors and various festival activities. http://en.summerjam.de/

Victoria Ska Fest – 1st week July (Victoria, BC) ~ One of the largest and longest-running ska festivals in the world, the Victoria Ska Fest is located on beautiful Vancouver Island in British Columbia. It features local & world-renowned ska bands as well as reggae, jazz, Latin, rock n roll, punk, soul and R&B. Produced by the non-profit 'Victoria BC Ska Society', VSF is dedicated to the preservation of ska. http://victoriaskafest.ca/

Antwerp Reggae Festival – 2nd week July (Antwerp, Belgium) ~ Smile! Antwerp Reggae Festival 'summer edition' produces an incredible line up of reggae, dancehall, ska, dub, rocksteady artists every year. This outdoor concert is quickly gaining popularity, and provides all the festival amenities such as a market vending, arts & crafts as well as Caribbean cuisines. http://www.antwerpreggaefestival.be/

Dub Camp Festival – 2nd week July (Le Pellerin, France) ~ Produced by the GetUp Association, this three-day eco-festival promotes environmental preservation while showcasing over 150 dub artists and sound systems from around Europe. Located at Le Pellerin, a protected site selected for its biodiversity, Dub Camp Festival attracts over 15,000 concert-goers, provides organic foods, arts & crafts and tent camping. https://www.dubcampfestival.com/

Oland Roots Festival – 2nd week July (Oland, Sweden) ~ Created in 2004, Oland Roots is a non-profit organization that produces this annual three-day reggae music festival in Sweden. Located in beautiful Haga Park on Brunnsviken Lake, this irie event offers award-winning international reggae and dancehall artists as well as showcasing the best local talent. It also offers a beer tent, Caribbean & international foods, camping and vendors. http://www.olandroots.com

One Love Reggae Festival – 2nd week July (Udine, Italy) ~ This five-day, fun-in-the-sun reggae festival hosts one of the best beach venues in Europe. Attracting the top reggae, dancehall, dub & world music performers, it provides a variety of regional, Jamaican & international cuisines, market vendors, camping, bungalow rentals, two swimming pools, volleyball, basketball, tennis & a children's playground. http://www.onelovefestival.it/

Soca Reggae Festival – 2nd weekend July (Winnipeg, Canada) ~ Since 2006, this irie three-day event has been showcasing the best regional and international reggae & Caribbean performers in downtown Winnipeg. This outdoor venue promotes the unity of all people, highlights Canada's multicultural community is fun for the entire family. http://www.socareggaefestival.ca/

Sunrise Reggae & Ska Festival – 2nd weekend July (Burtenbach, Germany) ~ One of the most intimate festivals in Germany, this irie event provides '3 Days of Peace & Love' while featuring the best local and international reggae, ska & dancehall artists. It includes an African Caribbean bizarre, arts & crafts, regional & international foods, dancehall tent, free camping & swimming. http://www.sunrisefestival.de/index.htm

Bayfront Reggae & World Music Festival – 3rd weekend July (Duluth, MN) ~ The largest festival in Minnesota, this event is a tribute and celebration to reggae and world music artists that promote 'love, hope and equality for all people worldwide'. Located on the water in Bayfront Festival Park, it offers a variety of market vendors, arts & crafts, local & international foods and artisan wares. http://www.bayfrontreggae.com/

Grace Jamaican Jerk Festival – 3rd weekend July (Queens, NY) ~ Known as the "Biggest Caribbean Food Festival in the USA", this annual culinary event produces Jamaican Jerk festivals nationwide to preserve its culinary authenticity. It also hosts some of the top reggae & soca artists today as well as helps support the local Caribbean communities of New York and surrounding areas. www.jerkfestivalny.com

One Love Gathering – 3rd weekend July (Valcea, Romania) ~ This free-of-charge reggae festival is located on the beautiful shores of Vidra Lake, and is supported solely by donations & volunteers. Started in 2009, it features local and regional reggae artists, vendors, foods, arts & crafts, cinema, campfires, workshops, and promotes respect, love and positive vibes for all people. http://onelovefestival.wordpress.com/music/

Oroville Rock Reggae JamFest – 3rd weekend July (Oroville, CA) ~ Produced by Stephen Marley, The Ghetto Youths & IFA Journey, this irie two-day reggae jamfest showcases legendary reggae & dancehall artists from around the world. Located on the river at the River Reflections RV Resort & Campground, this venue offers market vendors, Caribbean & international cuisine, arts & crafts, cultural activities, and provides abundant tent camping and RV parking. http://orovillerockreggaejamfest.com/

Rastaplas Festival – 3rd weekend July (Zoetemeer, Netherlands) ~ One of the premiere reggae festivals in the Netherlands, *Rastaplas* features upcoming artists combined with the top reggae, dancehall & world music stars to unite various cultures. It provides a huge selection of Jamaican, Caribbean & international cuisine, arts & craft vendors and various cultural festival activities. http://rastaplas.nl/

Reggae in Los Angeles – 3rd weekend July (Los Angeles, CA) ~ Brand new on the reggae festival circuit, this show breaks out of the gate hosting world-renowned reggae & dancehall artists. Located in the historic Wiltern Theater in downtown LA, this event is dedicated to bridging together all generational and racial differences, this music event promotes unity among all people through the love of reggae music. http://reggaeinla.com/

Reggae na Piaskach Festival – 3rd weekend July (Wielkopolska, Poland) ~ One of the most popular, open-air reggae festivals in Europe, this event promotes the best of Polish, Jamaican & international reggae artists. It is located at Lake Piaski offering recreational climbing, hiking, swimming, kids playground, and provides international & vegetarian food options. http://www.reggaenapiaskach.pl/

Reggae Night at Hollywood Bowl – 3rd weekend July (Hollywood, CA) ~ One of the most anticipated reggae shows in LA every year, this irie outdoor event attracts award-winning reggae, dancehall & world music artists. With incredible acoustics, the Hollywood Bowl is among the top concert venues in southern California and provides various local and international food options, market vending, and various concert amenities. http://www.hollywoodbowl.com/

Reggae Sumfest – 3rd week July (Montego Bay, Jamaica) ~ Replacing the once favorite *Reggae Sunsplash*, this week-long mega event is the largest music festival in Jamaica. It showcases a powerful lineup of legendary reggae, dancehall & world music performers, and holds true its motto of "Promoting Music, the Universal Force". There is a huge vendor market area with Jamaican, Caribbean & international cuisine and arts & crafts. http://www.reggaesumfest.com/2013/index.php/en/

Simmer Down Festival – 3rd weekend July (Birmingham, England) ~ This is Birmingham's largest international reggae festival, is free-of-charge, and showcases an incredible lineup of local & international reggae artists at Handsworth Park. This event is in its fourth year, and includes Jamaican, Caribbean & international cuisine, various festival vendors, arts & crafts, cultural activities as well as dance and education workshops. https://www.facebook.com/simmerdownfestival

Soul Rebel Festival – 3rd weekend July (Boulder, CO) ~ Located in the beautiful Rocky Mountains, this annual grassroots music festival features an array of music genres including roots reggae, world and afro-pop. This irie event offers local, regional & international foods, vendors, and promotes cultural harmony, awareness and understanding through conscious music and art. https://www.facebook.com/SoulRebelFestival

Dallas Nelson Mandela World Music Festival – 4th weekend July (Dallas, TX) ~ Named after the late South African President, this two-day outdoor festival celebrates the life, legacy and mission of Nelson Mandela. It features top reggae & world music performers, attracts a massive international audience and promotes on-site initiatives such as a food drive for feeding the hungry and education programs for children and adults. http://www.dallasmandelafest.com/

Foundation Reggae Festival – 4th weekend July (Xuvia, Spain) ~ This annual two-day music festival draws the best reggae and world music performers year after year. It provides a variety of Caribbean, European and international food options, a large vending marketplace, arts & crafts, and festival activities for the children. http://www.foundationreggaefestival.org/

Garance Reggae Festival – 4th weekend July (Bagnols-sur-ceze, France) ~ The premiere reggae festival in France, *Garance* showcases four days of legendary roots reggae, dancehall & world music artists. This massive event provides top-notch concert amenities such as regional, Jamaican & international food court, a huge market vending area, swimming and various festival activities. http://www.garancereggaefestival.com/

Northwest World Reggae Festival (NWWRF) – 4th weekend July (Marcola OR) ~ Featuring regional as well as international and world music artists, this irie festival is located on a private, campground that provides heated showers and over two miles of shady tent/RV camping. It boasts plenty of hiking trails, a natural green amphitheater, yoga & African dance classes, late night dancehall & organic food vendors, and is dedicated to its mission of "Reduce, Reuse, Recycle". www.nwworldreggae.com

Reggae Jam Festival – 4th weekend July (Bersenbrueck, Germany) ~ For over 20 years, Reggae Jam Festival has hosted the best reggae & dancehall artists from around the world. Held in Germany's beautiful Klosterpark, this three-day outdoor event features a large market vendor area, Caribbean and international foods, an on-site dubplate studio, sound tents, drum circles, camping, swimming & showers. http://www.reggaejam.de/home/

AUGUST

Jambana One World Festival – 1st weekend August (Ontario, Canada) ~ Produced by Jones & Jones Productions, this two-day outdoor reggae festival boasts the top reggae, dancehall, soca, calypso & world music artists. It offers a food village, health tents, children's activities, market vending, a domino tournament, comedy and a VIP section. http://jambana.com/

Ostroda Reggae Festival – 1st weekend August (Ostroda, Poland) ~ Ostrada is one of Poland's premiere music festivals featuring the best of reggae, dancehall and ska music. This three-day event offers multiple music stages, international foods, contests, dance workshops, educational meetings, exhibitions and various festival activities. http://www.ostrodareggae.com/

Reggae Geel – 1st weekend August (Geel, Belgium) ~ Beginning in 1978, *Reggae Geel* is one of the oldest reggae festivals in Europe and the largest in Belgium. Attracting over 30,000 visitors every year, this premiere event features world-renowned lineup of reggae, dancehall, ska, rocksteady and dub artists. It is also a 'Fair Trade Festival' that offers a large international food court and vendor area, as well as coffee & tea and fresh-squeezed juices, fresh water, tent camping, festival activities and various wi-fi hotspots for internet access. http://www.reggaegeel.com/nl

Reggae in the Park – 1st weekend August (Philadelphia, PA) ~ Presented by The Mann, AEG and Jamaican Dave Productions, this concert hosts the top reggae & dancehall artists from Jamaica and is located in beautiful Fairmont Park. It includes two stages, live DJ sets, arts & crafts, various market vendors and a great selection of Jamaican, Caribbean & international cuisine. http://manncenter.org/events/2013-08-04/beres-hammond-reggae

Reggae on the River – 1st weekend August (Piercy, CA) ~ Presented by the Mateel Community Center, ROTR is California's premiere three-day reggae festival showcasing the finest in reggae, dancehall & world music. This irie venue is located on the Eel River in green Humboldt County, provides tasty local and international foods, children's activities and numerous festival amenities. http://www.reggaeontheriver.com/

Reggae Sun Ska Festival – 1st weekend August (Aquitaine, France) ~ This is one of the largest festivals in France and features a variety of music genres including roots reggae, dancehall, dub & ska. This three-day event is located on the shores of Gironde River and is celebration of music, culture and unity. It boasts three different music stages, provides various local & international cuisines, vendors and numerous festival activities. http://www.reggaesunska.com/fr

Revolutionary Women & Reggae – 1st weekend August (Lawrence, MA) ~ Dedicated to Harriet Tubman, RWR is a tribute concert that highlights the countless contributions that women make in society. It showcases top female reggae & dancehall artists and promotes global guidance for all women. http://www.revolutionarywomenandreggae.com/

Uppsala Reggae Festival – 1st weekend August (Stockholm, Sweden) ~ The premiere reggae festival in Sweden, Uppsala attracts hard core roots reggae and dancehall fans from around the world. Besides hosting award-winning reggae & dancehall performers, it offers a variety of Caribbean and international cuisine, numerous festival activities and market vendors. http://www.uppsalareggaefestival.se/

Afrika-Karibik Festival – 2nd weekend August (Aschaffenburg, Germany) ~ With its motto "One Race Human", this four-day festival showcases a diverse selection of top reggae, dancehall & world music artists. It provides three music stages, a world bazaar, cultural accessories, a food court hosting over 20 African-Caribbean food options, drum groups, a relaxing beach area, a children's activity area and plenty of camping. http://www.karibik-festival.de/

Calgary ReggaeFest – 2nd weekend August (Calgary, Canada) ~ One of the largest reggae festivals in Canada, this event features the best Canadian & international reggae artists transcending cultural, musical and racial boundaries. It provides local and Jamaican food vendors, an incredible beer garden, cultural activities, arts & crafts and a separate paly area for children. http://www.reggaefest.ca/

Monterey Bay Reggae Festival – 2nd weekend August (Monterey, CA) ~ Located at the Monterey Fairgrounds, this is one of the longest running and most anticipated concerts in California. This music festival is dedicated to promoting peace and love through cultural music and a 'conscious community', and provides many festival amenities such as local organic and international cuisine, VIP area, Turf Club and arts & craft vendors. http://www.mbayreggaefest.net/

Overjam International Reggae Festival – 2nd weekend August (Tolmin, Slovenia) ~ Overjam is the largest reggae festival in Slovenia and is making its mark as a top venue on the reggae concert circuit. It features over 100 reggae, dancehall and world music artists from over 40 different countries across four music stages. Located on the beautiful Soca River, this venue offers Caribbean & international cuisine, market vendors, free camping, a large beach and kids area. http://www.overjamfestival.com/

Reggae Sundance Festival – 2nd weekend August (Liempde, Netherlands) ~ One of the premiere reggae festivals in Europe, RSF is an irie three-day, open-air event that hosts legendary reggae, dancehall & world music performances. Surrounded by over 200 acres of forest and recreation area, this venue provides camping, festival vendors, cultural activities as well as Jamaican & international food options. www.reggaesundance.nl

Six Flags Caribbean Concerts – 2nd weekend August (Jackson, NJ) ~ Trinifly Promotions presents this annual music concert series that showcases chart-topping reggae & dancehall artists from around the world. This highly anticipated event is located at the Six Flags theme park in NJ, and provides Caribbean cuisine, park vendors, VIP tickets and various transportation options to & from the show. http://www.caribbeanconcerts.com/

South Bend International Festival – 2nd weekend August (South Bend, IN) ~ One of the largest family-themed music events in Indiana, SBIF features some of the top local & international reggae artists today. This festival promotes 'Peace + Love + Unity', provides international foods, vendors, a beer garden, arts & crafts, drum circles, as well as activities for children. www.southbendinternationalfestival.com

WestSide Reggae Festival – 2nd weekend August (Danbury, CT) ~ Located in the beautiful Ives Concert Park at Western Connecticut State University, WRF hosts some of the best artists in reggae, dancehall & world music. This prestigious venue is surrounded by 40 acres of wooded forest, gardens and hiking trails, and offers international cuisine, market vendors, arts & crafts & children's activities. http://www.heartandsoulentllc.com/

Montreal International Reggae Festival – 3rd weekend August (Montreal, Quebec) ~ This this annual three-day event is one of the largest music festivals in Canada, and showcases world-renowned reggae, dancehall, dub calypso and R&B artists. Dedicated to the theme "Unite Against Violence", MIRF provides a large selection of Caribbean & international cuisine, market vendors, arts & crafts and festival activities for children. http://montrealinternationalreggaefestival.com

Rototom Sunsplash – 3rd week August (Benicassim, Spain) ~ Located just north of Valencia Spain, Rototom is the largest reggae festival in Europe featuring the absolute best in reggae, dancehall, soca and Caribbean music. Located on Harmony Beach, this stunning week-long festival promotes respect, unity & environmental awareness, provides a large vendor village, Jamaican & international foods, multiple activities, yoga, meditation, swimming etc. www.rototomsunsplash.com/en/

OneLove Festival UK – 3rd weekend August (Bedfordshire, England) ~ This three-day, family-friendly festival attracts many top reggae, dancehall and world music performers from around the world. Inspired by the 1978 "One Love Peace Concert, this irie venue offers international cuisine, market vendors, and an epic 'battle of the dubplates'. http://www.onelovefestival.co.uk/

Brevard Caribbean Fest – 4th weekend August (Cocoa, FL) ~ One of the largest annual reggae festivals in Florida, this event is located at the scenic Cocoa Riverfront Park and hosts top reggae, Caribbean & world music artists. It provides full concert amenities such as Caribbean & international foods, arts & craft vendors, festival activities, face painting and a bounce house for the kids. http://brevardcaribbeanfest.com/

Chiemsee Reggae Summer – 4th weekend August (Chiemsee, Germany) ~ This five-day mega fest showcases over 100 bands, 5 stages and features the best of the best in reggae, dancehall, world music, dub, electro and more. Located on beautiful Lake Chiemsee, this event provides a huge selection of regional, Jamaican & international cuisine, market vendors, arts & crafts, festival activities, tent camping, swimming & activities for kids. http://www.chiemsee-summer.de/

Rastafest: Rastafari Arts & Culture Festival – 4th weekend August (Toronto, Canada) ~ One of Canada's largest music festivals, this event promotes Rastafarian culture by showcasing local and international reggae, dancehall, dub poetry artists. Rastafest offers a variety of regional & international foods, African/Caribbean dance & drumming, market vending, cultural activities, visual arts and a youth talent show. https://www.facebook.com/pages/Rastafest/133720213499119

Reggae on the Rocks – 4th weekend August (Red Rocks Amphitheatre, Morrison, CO) ~ Presented by Bill Bass Concerts & Live Nation, this is one of the most anticipated reggae events on the concert circuit. Reggae on the Rocks features legendary reggae & world music artists in one of the world's most unique natural amphitheaters that produces extremely high-quality acoustics unlike any other venue. www.redrocksonline.com

SEPTEMBER

Unity Festival – 2nd weekend September (Guerneville, CA) ~ Located on the Russian River in Sonoma wine country, this three-day festival is dedicated to unifying the human spirit through music, culture, art, dance and education. It showcases top reggae & world music artists, and its proceeds are donated to charities that help abused children & disabled veterans. This event provides food vendors, arts & crafts, artisan wares, camping & late-night DJ's. http://www.unityfestival.com/

Arizona Reggae Fest – 4th weekend September (Lake Havasu, Arizona) ~ Founded by Will Davis & Doing Thangs Productions, this irie two-day festival features some of the top local, national and international reggae & world music performers. Located on beautiful Lake Havasu, it provides a festival market area including international foods, live art demonstrations, informational exhibits and various festival activities, with its proceeds donated to charities such as the Autism Society and St. Jude's Hospital in Phoenix. http://www.azreggaefest.com/

Long Beach Jerk Fest – 4th weekend September (Long Beach, CA) ~ Produced by Big Ship Music Inc., this southern California culture fest features the best roots reggae, dancehall, Latin & world music. Strategically located on the waterfront at Queen Mary Park in Long Beach, this show offers a great selection of Caribbean, Latin & international cuisine, market vendors, arts & crafts and various festival activities. Combining music, food and culture, this irie event celebrates peace, love & unity in the community and is an enjoyable day for the entire family. http://www.longbeachjerkfest.com/

OCTOBER

International Reggae & World Music Awards (IRAWMA) – 1st weekend October (Ft. Lauderdale, FL) ~ Founded by Ephraim M. Martin, this annual tribute concert recognizes, honors and celebrates the accomplishments and contributions of reggae, dancehall and world music artists. Located near the beach in Ft. Lauderdale, IRAWMA also travels to various cities worldwide to promote reggae music, Caribbean cultural and its impact on society. http://www.irawma.com/

NOVEMBER

4 Seasons Annual Party Cruise – 1st week November (Miami, FL) ~ All aboard Carnival Cruise Lines for this intimate irie reggae cruise experience. Featuring some of the top reggae, Caribbean & world music artists today, this five-day cruise offers a boatload of amenities including air-conditioned rooms, numerous dining options, salon, spa, fitness center, library, shopping mall, casino, comedy show, carnival youth programs, and a personalized meet & greet with your favorite reggae artists. http://www.4seasonspartycruise.com/

Grace Jamaican Jerk Festival – 1st weekend November (Sunrise, FL) ~ Located in the warm tropical breezes of Florida, this is the same irie culinary festival that is held on the 3rd week of July in Queens NY. *Jamaican Jerk Festival USA Inc*. produces Jerk festivals nationwide to promote and preserve Jamaican culinary authenticity. It also showcases some of the top reggae, soca & world music artists today as well as helps support local Caribbean communities. www.jerkfestival.com

DECEMBER

Ghetto Splash – 2nd weekend December (Kingston, Jamaica) ~ Produced by Shocking Vibes Productions and Downsound Records, Ghetto Splash has now returned after a long hiatus and is once again among the most anticipated concerts on the reggae calendar. Sponsored by Boom energy drink, this event features top reggae and dancehall artists, and proceeds of the show are donated to help inner city youths in Jamaica. It also offers festival amenities such as market vending, arts & crafts and Jamaican cuisine. https://www.facebook.com/BoomGhettoSplash

ONE Caribbean Music Festival – 2nd weekend December (Ft. Lauderdale, FL) ~ Hosted at Central Broward Regional Park, ONE Caribbean Music Festival is an irie two-day show that is growing in popularity! Produced by Art of Music Productions, this world-class event showcases top reggae and dancehall artists from around the Caribbean, and sponsors a One Toy Drive which encourages patrons to *bring an unwrapped gift as a gift to a child in the* Caribbean. http://onecaribbeanfestival.com/

Reggae Sting – December 26th (Portmore, Jamaica) ~ Dubbed 'the Greatest One Night Reggae & Dancehall Show on Earth', this high-energy musical extravaganza is held every year on December 26th (Boxing Day) in Portmore, Jamaica. It features veteran as well as upcoming reggae & dancehall artists in a live competition of chanting, toasting, singing and rapping against each other to win the champion crown of Reggae Sting. This incredible show is a MUST SEE for die-hard dancehall fans. http://www.bringthesting.com/

Cream of the Crop – 4th weekend December (Ocho Rios, Jamaica) ~ Produced by Purpleskunkz Entertainment, Cream of the Crop is the last major show of the year on the reggae circuit, and hosts the top 10 most established reggae and dancehall artists as well as emerging superstars. This premiere event is held every year in beautiful Ocho Rios, and offers a VIP section, festival vendors and a great selection of Jamaican & Caribbean cuisines. https://www.facebook.com/pages/Purpleskunkz-Entertainment/580434595308630

Festival	Date	Location
January		
Shaggy & Friends	1st weekend January	Kingston, Jamaica
Rebel Salute	3rd weekend January	St. Ann Parish, Jamaica
Jamaican Jazz & Blues Festival	4th weekend January	Kingston, Trelawny & Montego Bay
Panama Reggae Jam Music Festival	4th weekend January	Panama City, Panama
February		
Bob Marley Birthday Bash	1st weekend February	Negril, Jamaica
Dub Champions Festival	1st weekend February	Vienna & Amsterdam
One Love Festival	1st weekend February	Tauranga, New Zealand
9 Mile Music Festival	2nd weekend February	Miami, FL
Tribute to the Reggae Legends	President's Day, February	San Diego, CA
Blue Mountain Music Festival	3rd weekend February	Holywell, Jamaica
Oneness Reggae Fest	3rd weekend February	St. Mary, Jamaica
Ragga Muffins Festival	3rd & 4th weekend February	Bay Area & Long Beach, CA

Festival	Date	Location
March		
MoonSplash	2nd weekend March	Dune Preserve, Anguilla
April		
Austin Reggae Festival	3rd weekend April	Austin, TX
Easter Reggae Showcase	3rd weekend April	Brixton, London
Barbados Reggae Festival	4th week April	Barbados
Dis Poem Word Festival	4th weekend April	Portland, Jamaica
May		
Freedom Sounds Ska & Reggae Festival	1st weekend May	Cologne, Germany
Reggae on the Bay	1st weekend May	O2 Park, Trinidad
SoCal World Music Festival	2nd weekend May	Pala, CA
Gambia International Roots Festival	2nd – 3rd weekends May	Gambia, Africa
Buckroe Beach Reggae Festival	3rd weekend May	Hampton, VA
Best of the Best	4th weekend May	Miami, FL

Festival	Date	Location
May		
California Roots Festival	4th weekend May	Monterey, CA
Camp Reggae	4th weekend May	Turtle Town, TN
Four Roses Kentucky Reggae Festival	4th weekend May	Louisville, KY
UCLA Jazz Reggae Festival	4th weekend May	Los Angeles, CA
June		
City of Trees Reggae Music Festival	1st weekend June	Sacramento, CA
Jamming Festival	1st weekend June	Bogota, Columbia
Riddim Festival Aalborg	1st weekend June	Aalborg, Denmark
RUHR Reggae Summer	1st weekend June	Dortmund, Germany
Reggae in the Desert	2nd weekend June	Las Vegas, NV
Reggae in the Hills	2nd weekend June	Angel's Camp, CA
Aarhus Reggae Festival	3rd weekend June	Aarhus, Denmark

Festival	Date	Location
June		
Central Florida International Reggae Festival	3rd weekend June	Orlando, FL
Conscious Culture Festival	3rd weekend June	Tonasket, WA
Omaha Solstice Reggae & World Music Festival	3rd weekend June	Omaha, NB
Sierra Nevada World Music Festival	3rd weekend June	Mendocino, CA
Ziontific Summer Solstice Music Festival	3rd weekend June	Stockbridge, VT
Couleur Café Festival	4th weekend June	Brussels, Belgium
Groovin' in the Park	4th weekend June	Jamaica, Queens NY
Reggae in the Trees	4th weekend June	Selma, OR
St. Kitts Music Festival	4th weekend June	St. Kitts, WI
Sumol Summer Fest	4th weekend June	Ericeira, Portugal
Uplift Music & Arts Festival	4th weekend June	Greenfield, NH
Woodbury Reggae Festival	4th weekend June	Woodbury, CT

Festival	Date	Location
July		
Festival Musa Cascais	1st weekend July	Cascais, Portugal
Houston Caribbean Festival	1st week July	Houston, TX
International Festival of Life	1st week July	Chicago, IL
International Reggae Day	1st day July	Kingston, Jamaica
Lakesplash Festival	1st weekend July	Bern, Switzerland
Montenegro Sun Reggae Festival	1st weekend July	Petrovac, Montenegro
SummerJam Festival	1st weekend July	Cologne, Germany
Victoria Ska Fest	1st week July	Victoria, BC
Antwerp Reggae Festival	2nd weekend July	Antwerp, Belgium
Dub Camp Festival	2nd weekend July	Le Pellerin, France
Oland Roots Festival	2nd weekend July	Oland, Sweden
One Love Reggae Festival	2nd week July	Udine, Italy

Festival	Date	Location
July		
Soca Reggae Festival	2nd weekend July	Winnipeg, Canada
Sunrise Reggae & Ska Festival	2nd weekend July	Burtenbach, Germany
Bayfront Reggae & World Music Festival	3rd weekend July	Duluth, MN
Grace Jamaican Jerk Festival	3rd weekend July	Queens, NY
One Love Gathering	3rd weekend July	Valcea, Romania
Oroville Rock Reggae JamFest	3rd weekend July	Oroville, CA
Rastaplas Festival	3rd weekend July	Zoetemeer, Netherlands
Reggae in Los Angeles	3rd weekend July	Los Angeles, CA
Reggae na Piaskach Festival	3rd weekend July	Wielkopolska, Poland
Reggae Night at Hollywood Bowl	3rd weekend July	Hollywood, CA
Reggae Sumfest	3rd week July	Montego Bay, Jamaica
Simmer Down Festival	3rd weekend July	Birmingham, England

Festival	Date	Location
July		
Soul Rebel Festival	3rd weekend July	Boulder, CO
Dallas Nelson Mandela World Music Festival	4th weekend July	Dallas, TX
Foundation Reggae Festival	4th weekend July	Xuvia, Spain
Garance Reggae Festival	4th weekend July	Bagnols-sur-ceze, France
Northwest World Reggae Festival	4th weekend July	Marcola OR
Reggae Jam Festival	4th weekend July	Bersenbrueck, Germany
August		
Jambana One World Festival	1st weekend August	Ontario, Canada
Ostroda Reggae Festival	1st weekend August	Ostroda, Poland
Reggae Geel	1st weekend August	Geel, Belgium
Reggae in the Park	1st weekend August	Philadelphia, PA
Reggae on the River	1st weekend August	Humboldt, CA

Festival	Date	Location
August		
Reggae Sun Ska Festival	1st weekend August	Aquitaine, France
Revolutionary Women & Reggae	1st weekend August	Lawrence, MA
Uppsala Reggae Festival	1st weekend August	Stockholm, Sweden
Afrika-Karibik Festival	2nd weekend August	Aschaffenburg, Germany
Calgary Reggae Fest	2nd weekend August	Alberta, Canada
Monterey Bay Reggae Festival	2nd weekend August	Monterey, CA
Overjam International Reggae Festival	2nd weekend August	Tolmin, Slovenia
Reggae Sundance Festival	2nd weekend August	Liempde, Netherlands
Six Flags Caribbean Concerts	2nd weekend August	Jackson, NJ
South Bend International Festival	2nd weekend August	South Bend, IN
WestSide Reggae Festival	2nd weekend August	Danbury, CT
Montreal International Reggae Festival	3rd weekend August	Montreal, Quebec

Festival	Date	Location
August		
Rototom Sunsplash	3rd week August	Benicassim, Spain
OneLove Festival UK	3rd weekend August	Bedfordshire, England
Brevard Caribbean Fest	4th weekend August	Cocoa, FL
Chiemsee Reggae Summer	4th weekend August	Chiemsee, Germany
Rastafari Arts & Culture Festival	4th weekend August	Toronto, Canada
Reggae on the Rocks	4th weekend August	Morrison, CO
September		
Unity Festival	2nd weekend September	Guerneville, CA
Arizona Reggae Fest	4th weekend September	Lake Havasu, AZ
Long Beach Jerk Fest	4th weekend September	Long Beach, CA

Festival	Date	Location
October		
International Reggae & World Music Awards	1st weekend October	Chicago, IL
November		
4 Seasons Annual Party Cruise	1st week November	Miami, FL
Grace Jamaican Jerk Festival	1st weekend November	Sunrise, FL
December		
Ghetto Spalsh	2nd weekend December	Kingston, Jamaica
ONE Caribbean Music Festival	2nd weekend December	Ft. Lauderdale, Florida
Reggae Sting	December 26th (Boxing Day)	Portmore, Jamaica
Cream of the Crop	4th weekend December	Ocho Rios, Jamaica

~ Origins of Reggae Music ~

Reggae music has been a positive influence on society, culture, religion, politics and environmental awareness, and its origins are traced to traditional African & Caribbean culture. In the late 1800's, political leader, publisher and orator Marcus Mosiah Garvey predicted the 2nd coming of the Messiah would be crowned in Ethiopia. When Ras Tafari Makonnen, Haile Selassie I, was crowned emperor of Ethiopia in 1930, this was seen as the fulfillment of Marcus Garvey's prophecy, thus giving life to Rastafarianism. Haile Selassie's visit to Jamaica on April 21, 1966 furthered strengthened Rastafarian movement as over 100,000 people attended this spectacular event. The term *reggae* described a 'ragged' style of Caribbean music, and became synonymous with the Rastafarian movement.

Ska music originated in Jamaica in the late 1950's, and was the precursor to Rocksteady and Reggae music. It combined elements of Calypso & Caribbean with Jazz and R&B with a steady bass line and rhythms accented on the upbeat. Traditional ska bands featured drum & bass, rhythm guitars, keyboards and usually a 3-piece horn section consisting of a trombone, trumpet and saxophone. Clement "Coxsone" Dodd is one of the most important figures in ska history, as he recorded popular bands in his legendary Studio One that became extremely popular in Jamaica.

In addition to Coxsone Dodd, there were many early singers and studio producers that were vital to the success of ska and reggae music, including King Jammy, King Tubby, Augustus Pablo, Lee Perry, Toots & the Maytals, Jackie Mittoo, Lloyd Knibbs, Ruddy Redwood, Bunny Lee, Duke Reid, Errol Thompson, Prince

Jammy and Prince Buster to name a few. Formed by the Wailers in 1965, the Tuff Gong record label is where all of Bob Marley's reggae masterpieces were produced. Their positive music was instrumental in catapulting reggae to worldwide popularity by the early 70's.

Jimmy Cliff's 1973 film *The Harder They Come* further promoted Jamaican culture & music portraying a young man's struggles growing up in urban Jamaica. The film's soundtrack was loaded with reggae classics which helped Jimmy Cliff & reggae music to further expand to international audiences. By the mid 1970's, other reggae stars began to emerge such as Big Youth, Burning Spear, Black Uhuru, Dennis Brown, Gregory Isaacs, Steel Pulse, Sugar Minott, The Abyssinians, U Roy, Max Romeo, Horace Andy, Third World, Culture, Yellowman, Freddie McGregor, the Heptones, the Might Diamonds, the Gladiators, the Congos, and many others. Music labels like Studio One & Trojan Records were churning out consistent, high-quality albums that catapulted Bob Marley, Dennis Brown and others to unprecedented levels of international stardom. One of the most influential producers in reggae was Lee "Scratch" Perry from the Black Ark Studio in Jamaica, who worked extensively with Bob Marley and produced some of the best and most widely-acclaimed reggae albums of all time.

In the early 1980's, reggae music industry continued to evolve. Artists began singing more about conscious uplifting messages, ending racism and promoting unity among all people. Synthesized technology & sounds began to appear, with keyboards replacing horns and other instruments, and which produced a more digital sound while others retained the historical roots sound. In the mid 80's we saw singers like Yellowman,

Eek-a-Mouse and Tenor Saw gain worldwide fame. Dub music and dub poetry were also gaining notoriety at that time, becoming popular by artists like Linton Kwesi Johnson (LKJ) and Mutabaruka.

The 90's saw the emergence of dancehall superstars such as Buju Banton, Sizzla Kalonji, Capleton, Beenie Man & Bounty Killer. The new generation of dancehall artists are mashin' up di place today, including Mr. Vegas, Sean Paul, Shaggy, I-Octane, Konshens, Anthony B, Wayne Marshall, Lady Saw, Ninjaman, Delly Ranx, Exco Levy, Gappy Ranks, General Levy, Mavado, Vybz Kartel, Busy Signal, Aidonia, Spragga Benz, Wayne Wonder, Cham and Elephant Man to name a few.

Some of the top roots reggae artists today include Alpha Blondy, Tarrus Riley, Romain Virgo, Bushman, Luciano, Beres Hammond, Jah Cure, Kabaka Pyramid, Chronixx, Proteje, Pentateuch, Midnite, Barrington Levy, Tony Curtis, Tanya Stephens, Cali P, Dezarie, Richie Spice, Chezidek, and of course the Marley Brothers - Ziggy, Stephen, Damian, Ky-Mani, Rohan, Jo Mersa and Daniel Bambaata.

~ Charitable Reggae Organizations ~

1love.org – founded by the Marley family, its mission is to honor Bob Marley's vision 'for a better tomorrow' by supporting and donating to charities that share the same values, and uniting people by music to promote peace & love around the world.
www.1love.org

Ghetto Youths Foundation – founded by Ziggy, Stephen, Damian & Julian Marley, their mission is to provide relief for the poor.
http://ghettoyouthsfoundation.org/

Reggae Ambassadors Worldwide – an international network of dedicated reggae enthusiasts that help spread the positive message of reggae music.
http://www.reggaeambassadors.org/

Reggae for a Reason – founded by George "Fully" Fullwood, this organization hosts benefit concerts collection drives to help the homeless youth in Orange County & Los Angeles
http://www.reggaeforareason.org/

Rita Marley Foundation – based on the principle of love and compassion, this organization accepts donations and helps alleviate poverty and hunger in less developed countries.
http://www.ritamarleyfoundation.org/

Shaggy Foundation (Shaggy & Friends) – annual charity concert raising much needed funds for the Bustamante Children's Hospital in Jamaica.
www.shaggyfoundation.org

~ Protecting Africa's Elephants ~

Elephants around the world are being hunted and killed for their ivory tusks, and are on the endangered species list. Part of the proceeds of this book will be donated to help save & protect these majestic animals from extinction.

Burn The Ivory (Bend, OR)
http://burntheivory.org/

Dazzle Africa (Las Vegas, NV)
http://dazzleafrica.org/

Elephant Action League (Los Angeles, CA)
http://elephantleague.org/

International Fund for Animal Welfare (Yarmouth Port, MA)
http://www.ifaw.org

March 4 Elephants (San Francisco)
http://www.marchforelephants.org

Save The Elephants (Nairobi, Kenya)
http://www.savetheelephants.org/

SOS Elephants (Chad, Africa)
http://www.soselephants.org/

Tusk USA (New York, NY)
http://www.tuskusa.com/

~ Irie Reggae Resources ~

Irish & Chin – www.irishandchin.com

Jammin Reggae Archives – www.niceup.com

JamRockVybz – www.jamrockvybz.com

Jamstone Sound – www.jamstonesound.com

LargeUp – www.largeup.com

OutAroad – www.outaroad.com

Reggae Ambassadors Worldwide – www.reggaeambassadors.org

Reggae Festival Guide – www.reggaefestivalguide.com

Reggae Nation – www.reggaenation.com

Reggae Vibe – www.thereggaevibe.com

Reggaeville – www.reggaeville.com

Tuff Gong – www.tuffgong.com

World A Reggae – www.worldareggae.com

World Star Reggae – www.worldstarreggae.com

~ Listing of Reggae Artists ~

A

Aaron Silk

Abijah

Abja

Abyssinains

Addis Pablo

Admiral Tibet

African Head Charge

Afrikan Simba

Aggrovators

Aidonia

Akila Barrett

Alaine

Al Campbell

Alborosie

Alkaline

Alpha & Omega

Alpha Blondy

Alpha Steppa

Alpha Wess

Althea & Donna

Alton Ellis

Andrew "Bassie" Campbell

Andrew Bees

Andrew Diamond

Andrew Tosh

Anju Priest

Ansel Collins

Anthony B

Anthony Cruz

Anthony John

Anthony Malvo

Anthony Que

Anthony Red Rose

Apache Indian

Apple Gabriel

Archie Wonder

Arkaingelle

Army

Assassin

Aswad

Augustus Pablo

B

Baby Boom

Baijie

Bambu Station

Bankie Banx

Barrington Levy

Barry Brown

Bascom X

Basil

Beenie Man

Beres Hammond

Bernard Collins

Bescenta

Big Mountain

Big Youth

Bigga Haitian

Bim Sherman

Bingy Bunny

Bitty McLean

Blaak Lung

Black Crucial

Black I Am

Black Madhane

Black Roots

Black Ryno

Black Slate

Black Uhuru

Bob Andy

Bob Marley (& the Wailers)

Bobby Melody

Bounty Killer

Bramma

Brigadier Jerry

Boom Shaka

Bugle

Buju Banton

Bunji Garlin

Bunny Brissett

Bunny Ruggs

Bunny Lee

Bunny Wailer

Burning Spear

Burro Banton

Bushman

Busy Signal

Byron Lee

C

Cables

Cali P

Capleton King Shango

Carl Meeks

Carlene Davis

Carleton Livingston

Casper John

Ce'cile

Cedella Marley

Cedella Marley Booker (Bob Marley's Mother)

Cedrick Myton

Chaka Demus & Pliers

Chalice

Cham

Chantells

Charlie Chaplin

Cherine Anderson

Chevaughn

Chezidek

Chinese Man

Chino

Christafari

Christopher Ellis

Christopher Martin

Chris Wayne

Chronixx

Chuck Fenda

Chuckle Berry

Chuck Turner

Cimarons

Clancy Eccles

Clarendonians

Clint Eastwood

Clinton Fearon

Coco Tea

Collie Budz

Collin Levy

Comanche

Common Sense

Congo Ashanti Roy

Congos

Conrad Crystal

Cornell Campbell

Courtney John

Courtney Melody

Cultura Profetica

Cultural Roots

Culture

Cutty Ranks

D

Dallol

Dalton Browne

Damian Marley

Daniel Bambaata Marley

Danielle D.I.

Daville

Dawn Penn

Dean Fraser

Della Grant

Delly Ranx

Delroy Williams

Delroy Wilson

Demarco

Dennis Alcapone

Dennis Brown

Denroy Morgan

Derrick Morgan

Desi Roots

Desmond Dekker

Detour Posse

Dezarie

Dillinger

Dinquinesh

Doctor Alimantado

Don Carlos

Don Drummond

Donovan

Duane Stephenson

Dub Colossus

Dub Station

Dub Wise

E

Earl "Chinna" Smith

Earl 16

Earl Chinna Smith

Earl Zero

Earth & Stone

Easy Star All-Stars

Eccleton Jarrett

Echo Minott

Eddy Grant

Edi Fitzroy

Eek a Mouse

Elan

Elephant Man

Elijah

Elijah Prophet

Eljai

Empress Reggae

Empress Zana

Errol Dunkley

Etana

Ethiopians

Everton Blender

Exco Levi

F

Fanton Mojah

Flava McGregor

Foundation

Frankie Paul

Fred Locks

Freddie McGregor

Freddie McKay

Frisco Kid

G

Gappy Ranks

Garnett Silk

General Echo

General Levy

General Plough

General Trees

Gentleman

George "Fully" Fullwood

George Nooks

Ginjah

Gladiators

Glen Washington

Gondowana

Gramps Morgan

Gregory Isaacs

Groundation

Gussie Clarke

Gyptian

H

Half Pint

Heartafiya

Hempress Sativa

Heptones

Horace Andy

Hugh Mundell

I

Iba Mahr

Ijahman Levi

Ikaya

I-Kronik

Indiggnation

Ini Kamoze

Inka Inka

Inna de Yard

Inner Circle

I-Octane

Iration

I-Roy

Ishi Dube

Isiah Mentor

Israel Vibration

Itals

I-Threes

I Wayne

J

J Boog

J. C. Lodge

Jacob Miller

Jah9

Jah Bouks

Jah Cure

Jah Cutta

Jah Levy

Jah Mason

Jah Thomas

Jah Shaka

Jah Stitch

Jah Sun

Jahdan Blakkamoore

Jesse Royal

Jimmy Cliff

Jimmy Cozier

Jimmy Riley

Jo Mersa Marley

Joe Gibbs

Joe Higgs

John Brown's Body

John Holt

John McClean

Johnny Clarke

Johnny Osbourne

Joseph Hill

Josey Wales

Judy Mowatt

Julian Marley

Junior Braithwaite

Junior Brammer

Junior Delgado

Junior Kelly

Junior Marvin

Junior Murvin

Junior Reid

Junior Toots

Justin Hinds

K

Kabaka Pyramid

Kafu Banton

Katchafire

Kemar "Flava" McGregor

Ken Boothe

Kenyatta Hill

Kiddus I

Killer Bees

King Fragrance

King Jammy

King Zobbie

Kiprich

K'naan

Konshens

Kulcha Far I

Ky-mani Marley

L

Ladee Dred Yeshemebet

Lady G

Lady Saw

Lee "Scratch" Perry

Leroy Sibbles

Lieutenant Stitchie

Link n Chain

Linton Kwesi Johnson (LKJ)

Linval Thompson

Little John

Lloyd Brown

Lone Ranger

Long Beach Dub Allstars

Louie Culture

Love Joys

Luciano

Lucky Dube

Lui Lepke

Lutan Fyah

M

Macka B

Macka Diamond

Mad Cobra

Mad Professor

Majesty & the New Vibrations Band

Major Lazer

Marcia Griffiths

Marcia Higgs

Mark Wonder

Marlon Asher

Massicka

Matisyahu

Mavado

Max Romeo

Maxi Priest

Meditations

Melodians

Melody Makers

Michael Prophet

Midnite

Mighty Diamonds

Mikey Dread

Misty in Roots

Mojo Morgan

Morgan Heritage

Mr. Cheeks

Mr. Vegas

Mutabaruka

Mykal Rose

Mystic Dub

Mystic Revealers

Mystic Roots

N

Naâman

Nadine Sutherland

Nasio Fontaine

Naturalites

Natasja

Native Elements

Native Roots

Natural Black

Natural Vibrations

Nature

Nereus Joseph & the Sereus Band

Ninjaman

Noah Landale

O

Odel Johnson

Omar Perry

Omari Banks

Omari Edwards

Ooklah the Moc

Ossie Dellimore

Owen Gray

P

Pablo Moses

Pad Anthony

Papa San

Paragons

Parly B

Pato Banton

Pentateuch

Perfect Giddimani

Peter Broggs

Peter Lloyd

Peter Metro

Peter Spence

Peter Tosh

Petra

Phil Pratt

Phyllis Dillon

Pinchers

Popcaan

Pressure

Prezident Brown

Prince Alla

Prince Buster

Prince Far I

Prince Jazzbo

Prince Livijah

Prince Malachi

Prince Theo

Proteje

Puma Jones

Q

Queen Ifrica

Queen Makedah & the Sheba Warriors

Queen Omega

Quinto Sol

R

Raging Fyah

Rankin Scroo

Ranking Joe

Ras Attitude

Ras Batch

Ras Dem

Ras Henry

Ras Indio

Ras Michael & the Sons of Negus

Ras Midas

Ras Shiloh

Ras Zacarri

RasItes

Rastafarians

Ray Darwin

Ray "Wreckless" Simpson

Rebelution

Red Fox

Red Rat

Reggae Bubblers

Richie Campbell

Richie Davis

Richie Spice

Richie Stephens

Rita Marley

Robert Dallas

Robert Lee

Rocky Duwani

Rohan Marley

Roland Alfonso

Roman Virgo

Roots Nation

S

Sabe Tooth

Sagittarius Band

Samira

Sanchez

Santa Davis

Scientist

Scratchylus

Sean Paul

Shabba Ranks

Shaggy

Shan Hart

Singing Melody

Sister Carol

Sister Nancy

Sizzla Kalonji

Skatalites

Skrillex

Sly & Robbie

Smith & Mighty

SOJA (Soldiers Of Jah Army)

Soul Syndicate

Spanner Banner

Spragga Benz

Steel Pulse

Stephen Marley

Stephen Stewart

Sugar Minott

Sylford Walker

T

Tafari

Tami Chynn

Tamlins

Tanto Metro

Tanya Stephens

Tappa Zuckie

Tarrus Riley

Terry Linen

Tessanne Chin

Third World

Tiana

Tifa

Timberlee

Tippa Irie

Tommy McCook

Tony Chin

Tony Curtis

Tony Rebel

Tony Tuff

Toots & the Maytals

Tradesman

Tribal Seeds

Tribe of Judah

Trinity

Tristan Palmer

Turbulance

Twinkle Brothers

U

UB40

Urban Dread

U-Black

U Brown

U Roy

Upsetters

V

Viceroys

Vivian Jones

Vybz Kartel

W

Wailers

Wailing Souls

Ward 21

Warrior King

Wayne Jarrett

Wayne Marshall

Wayne Smith

Wayne Wonder

Willi Williams

Willie Lindo

Winston Clarke

Winston Jarrett

Winston McAnuff

Winston Reedy

X

X-Rays

Xkaliba

Y

Yabby You

Yami Bolo

Yasus Afari

Yaz Alexander

Yellowman

Yvad

Z

Zacheous Jackson

Zamunda

Zap Pow

Zareb

Zema

Ziggi Recado

Ziggy Marley (& the Melody Makers)

Zion Train

Zukie Joseph

One Love

One People

One Heart

One Aim

One Destiny

www.ingramcontent.com/pod-product-compliance
Lightning Source LLC
Chambersburg PA
CBHW041526090426
42736CB00035B/19